Shine On!

A grateful & guided journal

Shine On!

date started:

date finished:

Life happens! Now what?

How about gratitude & journaling. These are tools to put in your toolbox. Blank pages can be intimidating so we decided it would be awesome to create a guided journal.

Our hope is that this journal will provide the space to help you look a little deeper, smile, and maybe even have an aha moment! We started with a prompt to get you thinking. These come from our own personal journeys. We then provide space for guided writing, jotting notes, drawing, and questions to ponder. Express yourself in any way you want.

Thinking about gratitude can help with being more present throughout the day and finding moments to savor.

Suggestions on using this book:
1) bring a sense of curiosity
2) find a quiet spot
3) have 5 minutes or more to spend
4) pick any page - you do not have to go in order
5) just write and let it go - it doesn't have to be perfect, it's just for you!

We wish you well on your journey and hope this book helps you enjoy the ride.

Hop on... Hold on tight! It's a hell of a ride, but you have to throw your hands up in the air to really enjoy life.

What one thing (within my control) would make today great?

STOP & JOT

Can I whistle? Whistle a tune, if not, hum one.

Have you ever noticed the way trees and colors glow depending on the light? I wonder if we are the same?

I am grateful for...

THOUGHTS & THINGS

Sunrise or sunset?

I start strong. Then I start to fade. Then I say screw the journey, I just want to get there.

What can I appreciate about an obstacle I have overcome?

NOTES, THOUGHTS & QUESTIONS

What journey comes to mind?

It is all a matter of perspective. Dandelions; weed, a bouquet from your kids or food? You get to decide!

I am grateful for...

JOT A THOUGHT OR DRAW A FLOWER

What's my favorite flower?

When life is tough, sometimes you just need to dance it out.

What do I appreciate about the music I listen to?

What's my favorite song? When's the last time I danced? Dance it out now!

Sometimes you walk through poo. Don't just stay there and stomp in it! Walk through, clean the shit off and move on.

What positive quality do I really admire about myself?

Is there something I need to do to move on?

You'll find wonderful new adventures when you get off the path. Explore! You will be amazed (or lost). Make sure you have water.

I am grateful for...

JOT A THOUGHT OR DRAW YOUR FAVORITE PLACE

Beach or mountains?

Even after a shitty day, I wake up grateful that I have a new one.

What is one good thing that happened during the day?

NOTES, THOUGHTS & QUESTIONS

What happens when I smile?

It makes me laugh that the one thing that is constant is change. Nothing stays the same. Isn't it ironic?

I am grateful for...

What is the deciding factor between following a rule or not?

You are not as special and unique as you think you are.
We are more alike than different.

What positive qualities of a role model do I value?

Why me? Why not me? What makes me different from anyone else?

Your actions make a difference. "Do as I say, not as I do" never works.

I am grateful for...

POEMS & PONDERINGS

What do I do to let people know I love them?

Sometimes I have to remind myself to let it flow and let it go.

What can I appreciate about my appearance today?

VISIONS

What am I holding on to?

Having people to celebrate the good times and walk through the tough times is priceless. No need to do it alone.

I am grateful for...

Am I doing what I need to do to cultivate my relationships?

It is not a secret; kindness and compassion can make it a better world.

What is one act of kindness someone has done for me that stands out?

NOTES...

What are some random acts of kindness I might do?

If you are always trying to be "normal" you will never know how AMAZING you can be.

I am grateful for...

Can I roll my tongue? Can I flip my tongue over? Try it.

Love what you do and it won't seem like work. Hopefully it will pay the bills. If not, at least you will be happy.

What do I admire about the employees at the places I frequent?

Do I find meaning in my work?

Sometimes finding your small patch of sunshine among the clouds and lying in it can be rewarding.

I am grateful for...

Stilettos, flip-flops, sneakers or barefoot?

When you are talking to someone, make them feel important by giving them your full attention. Listening can be a superpower.

What is an old relationship that I am grateful for?

PAUSE & PONDER

What are my superpowers?

If this is as good as it gets, I'm doing ALRIGHT!

I am grateful for...

HOPES & DREAMS

Pause. Can I feel my heartbeat?

Can I feel my breath?

Trying to keep things pretty on the outside isn't as helpful as being honest and truthful about the inside. Not being honest with ourselves is when emotions build and come out in unhealthy ways.

What is an opportunity I have today that most people don't that I can appreciate?

THOUGHTS & THINGS

How honest and truthful am I?

It is easy to complain, but that doesn't really get you anywhere. The goal is to be in the solution.

I am grateful for...

Am I in the solution?

Walking or sitting. Just listen. Be in the moment. Connect.

What is one object I love? What do I love about it?

Favorite farm animal. Why?

Growth is about letting things go, not getting more.
Subtracting, not adding.

I am grateful for...

IDEAS

Write a mathematical equation that leaves me with less.

Stuff happens when we are young that molds us into who we are as adults. As adults, we have to look at what works and what doesn't work. This process is a little like doing a deep cleaning on the inside. Work at discarding those old habits and roles that don't serve you anymore.

What do I appreciate about my childhood?

What is one old habit I want to get rid of?

Sometimes when I'm off, I need to have a little bite to eat, drink a little water and go outside.

What food do I really appreciate and why?

WORDS & WONDERINGS

My favorite meal is…

A little something can turn into a big something so make sure your little somethings matter.

I am grateful for...

WRITE A LITTLE SOMETHING

Can I wiggle my ears? Wag my tail? Give it a try.

Set aside a time for you. You are important and worthy of the time AND you will be better for others.

What is something I am better at today than I was yesterday?

What do I enjoy doing in my free time?

Make conscious choices. Are your decisions bringing you closer to or farther from who you WANT to be?

What is a past experience that felt bad at the time that I can appreciate now?

NOTES

Who do I want to be?

Which is better for you? Walking or running? It depends if something is chasing you.

What is one thing I appreciate about my health?

STRENGTHS

What is my favorite exercise?

You can't be vulnerable and honest if you are always trying to keep up appearances. When you do that, the ego, not the true self, is running the show.

What is one thing I appreciate about my body?

VALUES & VISIONS

How do I keep up appearances?

There is no magic pill to make you feel better. You have to put the work in. That's the magic.

I am grateful for...

DRAW YOUR MAGIC PILL

What would my magic pill do?

Being kind and doing something for others with no strings attached is the best way to start feeling better.

What is an opportunity I've had with someone that has made me feel better?

FORGET ME NOTS...

Who can I reach out to today that may need a "lift"?

Does thinking about the good bring in the good? I don't know, but if I think about a particular color, that is all I see and notice. So I think I'm going to think about the good.

What is one thing I am looking forward to today?

LOOK & NOTICE

Pick a color, then look around. Where do I see it?

Sometimes we bark because we are afraid. Sometimes we bark because we want attention. Maybe we need to just ask for what we want.

I am grateful for...

FREE TO WRITE

Am I barking or asking?

Life happens. It's a journey. At times I feel like I am going through the same stuff, but I'm not. There's always another lesson to be learned.

I am grateful for...

MY JOURNEY

What seems to keep repeating itself in my life?

Is it persistence or insanity if you keep running into a wall? I think insanity if it's the same wall and persistence if it's different walls.

How can a perceived weakness of mine also be a strength?

CLUES & CUES

Insanity or persistence?

Growth opportunities SUCK when you are in the middle of them, but are AMAZING when you come out on the other end. Definitely worth the journey in hindsight.

What positive quality can I find within something I think will suck today?

THOUGHTS & THINGS

What growth opportunity am I in right now?

Sometimes you have to surrender to win.

I am grateful for...

SIGNPOSTS

I need to surrender...

If you are interested in change, try visualizing. Imagine the details of what you want, feel it as if you were there. This can be a powerful tool.

What scent do I find enjoyable?

INTENTIONS

What's something I can try visualizing?

Sometimes you just need to start a meal with dessert.

I am grateful for...

JOT A THOUGHT OR DRAW SOMETHING SWEET

What is my favorite dessert?

Sometimes it takes a lot of pain and suffering to bring about the willingness to change. This willingness is just the beginning of the transformation and can feel unbearable. It will be worth the time and effort.

What is one change that has transformed my life?

PAUSE & PONDER

Is there anything I'm ready to change?

You alone are ENOUGH. You have nothing to prove to anybody.

I am grateful for...

MY STRENGTHS

What character/role am I playing in this world?

Are you ok living on the surface of life, just skating by?
If you are, that's ok, but I have a secret: when you look
deeper, life becomes more meaningful and rewarding.

What am I grateful for that I learned in school?

POEMS & PONDERINGS

Did I learn how to skate? Rollerblade?

What time is it? It's game time! **NOW** is the time to focus.

I am grateful for...

FOCUSED WRITING

Go BIG or Go HOME?

If I want to do something badly enough I will find a way to get it done. If I'm not getting it done, maybe I need to look at if I really want to do it. If I do, how can I make it happen?

What 3 things am I proud of?

IDEAS

What is holding me back?

When you share with others, it opens up a space for them to share. It helps to know that we all go through tough times and are not unique in our struggles.

What positive qualities have I picked up from my friends?

OPEN SPACE

What do I need to share?

A nice way to start your day with gratitude is simple.
Open your eyes and say thank you for this new day.

I am grateful for...

OPENING MY EYES

What is my morning routine?

We don't learn from just the experience. We learn from reflecting on the experience.

What did I appreciate about a former job?

EXPERIENCES

What did I love to do as a kid?

Do all those healthy things really work? I don't know.
Isn't it worth giving it a shot and see?

What do I appreciate about the food I ate (or didn't eat)
today?

STOP & JOT

What are the healthy things I do for me?

Celebrate you and celebrate others. It's important, it feels good and it's fun!

I am grateful for...

SONGS TO CELEBRATE

What am I going to celebrate?

When the clouds break, sometimes you take a chance to get outside. Sometimes the clouds come back and you get caught in the rain. Then what? You get wet. Regardless, all is well.

What do I appreciate about the outdoors?

When was the last time I walked in the rain?

"If it's not my way it's the highway." That makes for a lonely drive.

I am grateful for...

ROAD TRIP

What do I dig my heels in on?

Forgiving allows me to grow. Resentment only holds me back. It does nothing to the other person.

What do I appreciate about the people in my life?

Is there someone (or something) I need to forgive?

Understanding that we are all just doing the best we can helps grow compassion.

What do I appreciate about the country I live in?

COMPASSION

What character trait do I have that may push people away?

Walking up a hill is challenging but beneficial. It gets you stronger. It's the same with life's challenges - as long as you keep walking.

I am grateful for...

WINS

What do I need to walk through?

If you feel stuck, heavy or overwhelmed, stand up and shake it out. You might feel goofy, but it will get things flowing.

What sight did I see yesterday that I found enjoyable?

It's time to shake it out because I'm stuck on...

What's the story I am telling myself? Is it true? "I'm just the way I am" can be a big excuse for not changing behavior. I need to understand that I have the option to change if I want to .

I am grateful for...

MY STORY

What's my big excuse?

What does love have to do with it? It has EVERYTHING to do with it!

What gives me joy?

EVERYTHING!

What do I love to do?

When I'm in a bad place, I know that it will pass. YEA!
When I'm in a good place, I know that it will pass.
BUMMER!

I am grateful for...

PAUSE & PONDER

What needs to pass?

Less is ALWAYS more. Things weigh you down.

What is one piece of clothing I appreciate?

LET IT GO

Is there anything weighing me down?

We are all beautifully imperfect. It's the crack in the vase that lets the light in.

I am grateful for...

BEAUTIFULLY IMPERFECT

How does my light shine?

Don't just stop and smell the roses. Look and be amazed at the miracles all around you.

What do I appreciate about the home I live in?

SMELLING THE ROSES

What do I see around me right now?

You don't just go out and run a marathon. You break it down into tiny steps and build on them. Next thing you know, you are able to run a marathon. How can you use that in life?

I am grateful for...

TINY STEPS

What is the next step in what I want to do?

If I take away trying to be perfect, I find I enjoy things more.

What do I appreciate about my not-so-perfect self?

PERFECTLY IMPERFECT

What would I do if no one was watching?

Sometimes when I don't feel good, I just need to be. Sit with it and try not to fix it, just BE. That's hard.

What do I enjoy about quiet times?

What activities keep me busy?

Forgive. Holding onto resentments leaves you stuck in the past. Every time you think about a past hurt you are re-living the experience in the now.

I am grateful for...

FACTS & FICTION

What has been my biggest obsession this year?

If I stink, I want somebody to tell me nicely because I'm not always aware. We have to be there for each other. We are in this together.

What are 3 things that I savor

WISHES

Who is my go-to person?

Saltwater cures everything. Find your saltwater.

I am grateful for...

SWEET & SALTY

What gives me energy?

Everything passes. Bad things pass and unfortunately good things pass. Holding on tight and clinging doesn't help. Got to go with the flow or get stuck in the muck.

What is a learning experience I am grateful for?

FREE FLOW

How do I unstick myself?

Reach out and connect. It does the heart good.

I am grateful for...

HEART HAPPY

What 2 people can I reach out to this week?

I used to be scared of going down that dark hole. I thought once I went there I wouldn't be able to come out. When I went in I actually found there was a light at the other end.

I am grateful for...

LIGHT & DARK

What made me smile today?

It is not always all or nothing - there is a middle ground.

What do I appreciate about this moment?

CHANGES

What is the biggest change I've made this year?

Now that I know better, I DO better.

What type of art do I appreciate and why?

DOODLES & DOO-DADS

Where do I want to DO better?

Healthy habits don't keep me from having bad or tough days, but they do help me to make it through the tough times. That's why I want them to be habits.

I am grateful for...

JUMP AROUND

What are my healthy habits?

Do no harm. Some days, that is the best I can do.

What qualities do I appreciate in a co-worker?

LOVE & LAUGHTER

What gave me the biggest laugh this year?

Don't negate, compare or minimize how you are feeling. What you are feeling is yours to feel and is real. Walk through and work with it.

I am grateful for...

What emotions am I feeling right now?

Looking at the ocean and watching the waves reminds me I'm only one small drop in this big universe. I'm important, but no more than anyone else.

What is my favorite place and what do I appreciate about it?

DRIPS & DROPS

Where do I find my perspective?

One minute of meditation allows me at least one minute of stillness. I think that's a win.

What 3 things do I love to do?

What new skill do I want to learn?

Isolation is not a good thing, regardless of if we like it or not. Introvert or extrovert, we are social creatures.

I am grateful for...

Am I an introvert or extrovert?

Sometimes when you are feeling down, you just need to look up.

What lifts me up?

LOOKING UP

What is the best gift I have received?

I have to remember to get out of my head and get started. Take a small action. It does not have to be perfect, just start the process. Be willing to try something new.

I am grateful for...

ROCK & ROLL

What 2 compliments do I often get?

No matter your age, you can always have that twinkle in your eye. You might have to do grown up things, but in your heart you never have to grow up.

What do I appreciate about my playful side?

FUN & FABULOUS

What makes me twinkle?

Exercise makes you feel better. Naps are glorious.
Practice both in moderation.

I am grateful for...

DRAW YOUR FAVORITE ANIMAL

Favorite pet names?

I like the path I'm on - I don't always like myself on the path - but the path is good.

What do I appreciate about the direction my life is going?

What unexpected obstacle happened recently?

Planning for the future is important, but don't forget about the now. Enjoy the moment. Nothing is guaranteed.

I am grateful for...

IN THE MOMENT

What is my secret magic power?

What you think MATTERS, so be aware of what you focus on.

What do I appreciate about where I live?

FOCUS

What is my most precious possession? Why?

Usually when I'm uncomfortable with something I find that I'm in the middle of a growth opportunity.

I am grateful for...

GROWTH

What is my favorite family memory?

Take the time to be present and see how much more entertaining and interesting things can be.

What aspect of my personality am I grateful for?

NOTES, THOUGHTS, & QUESTIONS

What is the most adventurous thing I've ever done?

Be responsible for the energy you bring to a situation. Anger + Anger = Double Anger. We don't want to feed the beast. Instead, meet anger with love. It doesn't create a kumbaya moment, but it does help defuse the situation.

I am grateful for...

AHA!

What do I do when I get angry?

Allow yourself to get quiet so you can feel your inner voice/intuition. You already have the answers.

What do I appreciate about my intuition?

INNER VOICE

What is the best advice I heard this year?

Why is everybody drawn to water? Just sitting and watching it is mesmerizing. I think it's the movement that we are all secretly looking for. Can you imagine being in that flow? Wow!

I am grateful for...

When do I experience flow?

You have to look in order to see.

What do I appreciate about my senses?

DRAW THE FIRST THING THAT CATCHES
YOUR EYE

What am I looking at?

You can't always control what happens in your life, but you ALWAYS have a CHOICE in how you respond.

I am grateful for...

CHOICES

What is my most embarrassing moment?

Knowledge is awesome. Now take a step toward action.

What are 3 things I know for sure?

READY, SET, GO

What is my favorite movie? Why?

I have a strong forgettery. I forget when things were bad, and I forget when things were good. I guess I need to appreciate the moment for what it is, because clearly, I won't remember.

I am grateful for...

THINGS FORGOTTEN & REMEMBERED

What is my favorite song?

Noticing small things can actually open up a bigger picture.

What am I grateful for noticing today?

OPEN SPACE

What is my favorite book?

I never have to go through anything alone. Talking with my friends takes away the weight of the problem. It doesn't solve it, but it helps with the process.

I am grateful for...

TOGETHER

Who are my tribe of people?

It is tough to know when you just need to sit and be patient or when you need to do something. How do you decide? You have to ask for guidance.

I am grateful for...

LOVE & GUIDANCE

Who is the most inspiring person I have met?

Keep pushing through the tough stuff. It's on the other side that the miracle happens. This includes exercise and life.

What situations am I grateful I pushed through?

What 3 things are always on my to-do list?

Connect! Small gestures make a big difference. Just looking someone in the eye, nodding your head and smiling can brighten the day. I see you!

What do I appreciate about how I show up in the world?

I SEE YOU

Have I smiled at someone today?

Mood follows action. When I'm not feeling good, I need to do those things that help regardless of if I want to or not.

I am grateful for...

REFLECTIONS

One word to describe this adventure...

When the world shut-down for the Coronavirus (COVID-19) in March of 2020, Ann and Bonnie decided to start working on a retirement plan. The most important thing was to move to the beach!

After brainstorming, the 2 ideas that stood out for both were writing a gratitude book and animals. So, they got to work! Ann came up with many of the prompts on her walk to Bonnie's to work on the journal. Nature is a true inspiration.

Little by little they printed out the sayings and began gluing them into an old sketch book - adding the gratitude section, notes and questions. Once all was in place, Ann created the different graphics to add some flair.

This process has led them to create a new business adventure, Heart Space Creations LLC, that will include paper-strip art, personalized pet silhouette prints and maybe even another gratitude journal. The future is full of possibilities!

Ann and Bonnie can be contacted at abheartspace@gmail.com and at their etsy.com store: ABHeartSpace.

Follow us on Instagram: @HeartSpaceCreationsLLC

Ann Ellen is a middle school teacher with a MA Ed. She was born in eastern North Carolina and attended East Carolina University. She currently lives in the Northern Virginia area. She is always ready for celebrations and new adventures!

Bonnie Riley-Porter is a Professional Organizer and Life Coach. She was born and raised in Rockville Center NY and attended the University of Scranton in PA. She lives in Northern Virginia with her husband Steve and 2 dogs, Lula & Lucy.

We would like to thank our family and friends for cheering us on and a special thanks to Kathy McCloud, Suzanne Adler and Susan Dery for editing our mistakes.

CPSIA information can be obtained
at www.ICGtesting.com
Printed in the USA
LVHW081625210820
663747LV00009B/295